Chasing TORNADOES

by Becky Gold

Modern Curriculum Press

Parsippany, New Jersey

Credits

Illustrations: 10, 11, 14–15, 18, 19, 31, 32, 39, 42: Carlyn Iverson.

Photos: All photos © Pearson Learning Group unless otherwise noted. Front & back cover: A. & J. Verkaik/The Stock Market. Title page: Chris Johns/Tony Stone Images. 5: Randy Wells/Tony Stone Images. 6: t. ©Arvil A. Daniels/Photo Researchers, Inc.; b. ©H. Bluestein/Photo Researchers, Inc. 7: E.R. Degginger/Color-Pic, Inc. 8–9: ©H. Bluestein/Photo Researchers, Inc. 12: t. Timothy Marshall; b. Warren Faidley/International Stock. 13: t.. Timothy Marshall/Liaison International; m. Warren Faidley/International Stock; b. Timothy Marshall. 16: Warren Faidley/International Stock. 20–21: Brown Brothers. 22: Loew's Inc./Brown Brothers. 23: David James/Warner Bros./Universal/The Kobal Collection. 24: Chris Johns/Tony Stone Images. 25: Chris Johns/Tony Stone Images. 26: t. ; b. Timothy Marshall. 27: t. ; m. ; b. Timothy Marshall. 28: Peter Rauter/Tony Stone Images. 29: t. Charles Edwards/Cloud 9 Tours; b.0 PhotoDisc, Inc. 30: Peter Tenzer/International Stock. 33: ©David R. Frazier/Photo Researchers, Inc. 34: ©David R. Hardy/Science Photo Library/Photo Researchers, Inc. 35: David Young-Wolff/PhotoEdit. 36–37: U.S. Gov't Commerce Nat'l Severe Storms Laboratory/NGS Image Sales. 37: Gary A. Conner/PhotoEdit. 38: Annie Griffiths Belt/Corbis. 40: Bill Kreykenbohm/Virtual Images. 41: Teresa Hurteau/AP/Wide World Photos. 43: Reuters/Pete Silva/Archive Photos. 44: Pierre DuCharme/Ledger/Silver Image Photo Agency. 45: Reuters/John Kuntz/Archive Photos. 46: Bob Daemmrich. 47: Bob Daemmrich.

Cover and book design by Liz Kril

ISBN 0-7652-0881-4

Printed in the United States of America

7 8 9 10 11 12 13   07 06 05 04 03 02

1-800-321-3106
www.pearsonlearning.com

Contents

For Jane—a friend in all weather

Chapter

 Twister Trouble

The day starts out dry and quiet on the Kansas plains. In the afternoon the wind starts to blow. It brings wet air from the south.

A big dark cloud builds in the sky far away. As the cloud moves closer, it grows taller and darker. The wind blows harder. Lightning flashes. Thunder rumbles. A storm is coming!

Lightning

Hail stones next to baseball and golfball ▶

Now, the whole sky is dark gray, green, and purple. Rain begins to fall. Soon it turns into hail. The hard balls of ice bounce on the ground.

The wind grows stronger. It begins to spin round and round. It roars like a freight train coming closer and closer.

The wind whirls so fast that it forms a funnel shape under the clouds. The funnel looks like a rope as it reaches down toward the ground.

When the funnel touches the ground, the wind begins to push it. It weaves back and forth. Now it begins to move in a zigzag path. The funnel hits a tree and blows it over. The leaves are caught in the wind. They fly high into the sky.

A tornado is born.

Severe tornado ▶

Waterspout tornado ▶

Tornadoes are some of the strongest storms on Earth. They are often called twisters because of their twisting, turning winds.

Each tornado is different. The funnel cloud may be red, black, gray, white, or even clear. The color depends on the dirt, debris, or water the tornado picks up as it moves.

Usually only one tornado comes from a cloud. Sometimes several tornadoes form.

When tornadoes touch the ground, some may stand still. Others may race forward at 70 miles an hour.

Tornadoes may be narrow or almost two miles wide. They may last only a few minutes or go on for hours.

How do these strange storms begin?

DID YOU KNOW?

Some people call tornadoes cyclones. The word *cyclone* comes from a Greek word that means "to circle around" or "to whirl."

Chapter 2

The Life of a Tornado

Tornadoes start with warm, wet air. When the warm air meets cold air, the cold air pushes the warm air up. High clouds form. Then dry air blows in from another direction. It bumps into the wet air. The wind starts to rotate, or turn.

As the wind grows stronger, it blows up and down as well as around. It forms a column of air called a vortex. As the vortex spins faster, it stretches and becomes longer. Finally, it forms a funnel shape that moves down to the ground.

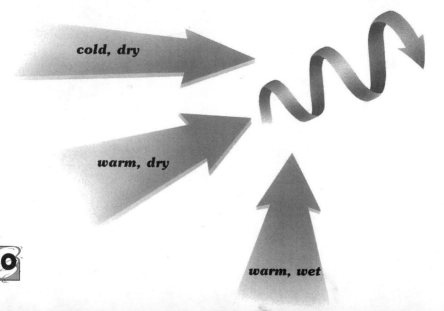

cold, dry

warm, dry

warm, wet

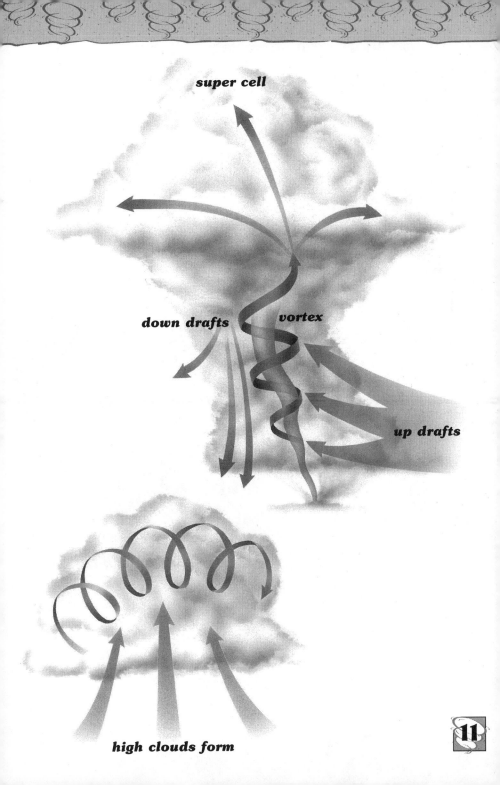

super cell

down drafts   vortex

up drafts

high clouds form

11

Tornadoes develop in stages. At first the funnel cannot be seen. As soon as it hits the ground, dust swirls up. This is the first stage of the tornado.

Stage 1

Stage 2

The second, or organizing stage starts when the funnel appears. Then the tornado begins to grow. The wind makes it move.

In the third, or mature stage, the tornado is strongest. Winds may blow at speeds of 250 miles an hour or more. The tornado acts like a big blender as it moves. Everything in its path is picked up or blown down.

Stage 3

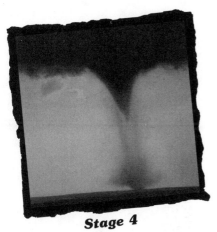

Stage 4

The fourth stage is called shrinking. The funnel begins to shrink, or become smaller. It may even tip to one side.

Finally, the vortex stretches thinner and thinner. The tornado loses touch with the ground and unwinds. This is the fifth, or decaying stage.

Stage 5

As many as 1,000 tornadoes occur in the United States every year. Most of them happen in an area of flat land called Tornado Alley. This area runs through Texas, Oklahoma, Kansas, Nebraska, Louisiana, Arkansas, Missouri, Iowa, North and South Dakota, Minnesota, and into Canada.

North Dako

**Sou
Dako**

Nebra

K

Texa

***Tornado Alley* runs up the
middle of the *United States*.**

14

However, tornadoes can happen anywhere. Mississippi, Alabama, Georgia, South Carolina, and Florida are often hit. Even Maine, New York, and Massachusetts have recorded tornadoes.

Some tornadoes have more power than others. Scientists rate how powerful tornadoes are with the Fujita-Pearson (foo jee tah - PEER sun) Scale. This scale lists the speeds of tornado winds and the damage they can do. The ratings start at F0, the weakest tornado. They go up to F5, the strongest tornado ever recorded.

Tornado debris ▼

- An **F0 tornado** (winds of 40–72 miles per hour) is very weak. It can break off tree branches.

- An **F1 tornado** (73–112 miles per hour) is weak. It can push cars off the road and take off roofs.

- An **F2 tornado** (113–157 miles per hour) is strong. It can uproot large trees and lift buildings.

- An **F3 tornado** (158–206 miles per hour) is severe. It can lift cars and roll them.

- An **F4 tornado** (207–260 miles per hour) is devastating. It can pick up houses and throw cars.

- An **F5 tornado** (261–318 miles per hour) is the strongest tornado recorded. It can throw houses and vehicles even farther than an F4.

DID YOU KNOW?

Tornado season is usually in the spring and early summer. This is the time when the weather "changes" from the cold winter to the warmer spring.

Chapter

Strange but True

Because of the way tornadoes move, they can do strange things. Only one house on a street may be damaged. A whole forest of trees might be snapped and broken except for one tree left standing and unhurt.

Over the years, people have told many strange stories about what tornadoes have done. Here are just a few of the odd things people have seen.

A tornado carried a lit kerosene lamp from a wrecked barn. It was set down about a third of a mile away. The lamp was still lit.

A tornado once carried a pair of pants 39 miles. The pants were found with $95 still in one pocket.

A recent F2 tornado in Iowa picked up a doghouse. It dropped the doghouse upside down a few blocks away. The dog was still inside. It was dazed but not hurt.

The tornado that hit Great Bend, Kansas, in 1915 carried away five horses from a barn. They were found unhurt a quarter of a mile away, still hitched to a rail.

Outside of Great Bend, the same tornado quietly took a roof off a house. The family didn't even know their roof was gone. They went outside to see what had happened to a neighbor's house. Then they noticed that their roof was missing.

The 1915 tornado also picked up other light objects. They were dropped over hundreds of miles. Along an 80-mile path, farmers found photographs, money, clothing, roof shingles, and book pages. A check someone wrote was found in a cornfield 305 miles away.

In 1931, a Minnesota farmer watched from the doorway of his barn as a twister lifted a train right off its tracks. Then the twister picked up his barn! The farmer wasn't hurt.

The fastest and worst tornado in United States history so far is known as the Tristate Twister. It traveled across Illinois, Indiana, and Missouri on March 18, 1925.

Most tornadoes last only a few minutes. The Tristate Twister lasted almost four hours. It moved in a straight path across 219 miles of land. It left a trail of broken barns and ripped-up fields. Ten towns were hit.

The greatest number of tornadoes at one time happened on two days in April in 1974. At that time, 148 tornadoes raced across 13 states.

A tornado carries Dorothy to the land of Oz where she meets the Scarecrow.

Some of the strangest things tornadoes have done happened only in books and in movies. Everyone knows these stories are not true. Yet they are fun to read and to watch.

One such tornado happens in *The Wizard of Oz*. In the book and in the 1939 movie, a young girl named Dorothy has a dream. Her house is lifted up by a cyclone. She and her dog, Toto, are carried with the house to a magical place called Oz.

Dorothy sees many strange things as she rides in the tornado. Cows fly past her window! Even a man in a bathtub blows by!

In the 1996 movie *Twister*, scientists chase tornadoes in Oklahoma. They have with them a special machine called Dorothy. The machine is named after the character in *The Wizard of Oz*. They want to put this machine in the path of a tornado. If the machine is picked up, they can gather scientific information about the tornado. The scientists hope to use what they find out to help know when tornadoes are coming. If people have time to find shelter, lives can be saved.

After several tries, the scientists set the machine in the path of an F5 tornado. The powerful twister picks up the machine. It nearly sweeps away the scientists too.

Scene from the 1996 movie "Twister"

Scientists struggling with equipment

The tornado in the movie *Twister* was not real. It was made on a computer. However, the scientists in the movie were based on real-life storm chasers.

DID YOU KNOW?

Scientist Charles Edwards developed a machine with two video cameras to film a tornado. Other instruments measure wind speed, temperature, and air pressure. He calls his machine the "Dillo-Cam" because it looks like an armadillo. In 1997, Dillo-Cam was successfully placed in the path of a tornado.

Storm Chasers

Storm chasing is a difficult job. Most tornadoes touch down on the ground for only a few minutes. Many tornadoes happen at night. So, just finding a tornado is hard to do.

Some storm chasers are scientists. Many of them are ham radio operators. Others are just people who think tornadoes are amazing. These chasers take many risks to track storms and learn how tornadoes work. They also help to warn people that a tornado is on the way.

Storm Chasers

Because tornadoes can be so dangerous, safety is important. The National Weather Service has programs to train storm chasers.

After training, storm chasers work in teams. They share information and ideas. They figure out safe ways to track storms by car and on foot.

A storm chaser's day might start with listening to a special weather radio. He or she wants to find out where big storms may be.

Tracking a storm ▲

Storm chaser van ▲

In groups the chasers drive to where the action is. The person at the wheel works on driving safely. Others watch computer screens.

Inside the storm chaser van ▲

They also listen to weather reports.

Storm chasers follow the storm clouds for hours. They may travel hundreds of miles. By the end of the day, they do not always find a tornado. They may not even find a storm.

Storm chasers on the road ▼

Driver's special equipment ▲

Besides tornadoes, storm chasers face other weather dangers. They may drive through heavy rain and hail. They also have to watch out for lightning during a storm.

When they see a tornado, chasers have to be careful not to get too close. The twisting winds can easily turn over a car. The winds also will pick up and toss heavy objects across a road or onto a car.

The tornado itself can change direction with no warning. One group of chasers reported that a tornado turned around and came right across the road between two of their cars!

A western tornado

By getting close to tornadoes, storm chasers learn how storms work. They share what they learn with their communities and with the National Weather Service. Tornadoes can form and move very fast. The more people know about what tornadoes do, the safer they will be.

Storm chaser's ad from the Internet

DID YOU KNOW?

Adults who want to know what it is like to chase a tornado can call a company that organizes storm chase trips. People pay these companies money to take them on storm chases. The company owners do not promise that people will see a real tornado.

Chapter

Tracking Weather

Scientists who study weather also watch out for big storms that might turn into tornadoes. These scientists are called meteorologists.

Weather forms in the atmosphere. This is the layer of gases that surrounds Earth. Meteorologists study the atmosphere. They measure temperature to find out how cold or hot the air is. They also want to know how wet or dry the air is. They look at wind speed, too. Air pressure is important as well. This is the force of the atmosphere pressing down on Earth. They watch the weather as it changes. Then they use what they know to predict what might happen next.

Meteorologist

Earth's atmosphere

31

Some meteorologists work for the National Weather Service and the National Severe Storms Forecast Center. They gather information about storms from hundreds of surface weather stations across the United States. Each station has its own special equipment to find and track storms.

Some of this special equipment measures different parts of the weather.

- Barometers measure air pressure. They alert scientists to changes in the atmosphere that could produce storms.

- Thermometers show the temperature of the air.

- Weather vanes show which way the wind is blowing – north, south, east, or west – and from which direction the weather is coming.

Storms are also tracked from the sky. Special weather balloons are sent up. They rise hundreds of feet to record information on temperature, how wet the air is, and air pressure. This information helps to show where a tornado might start.

◀ *Scientist releasing a weather balloon*

33

Weather satellites travel high above the earth. They take pictures of the atmosphere below. They show where the thickest clouds are. This is where storms are most likely to develop.

Another instrument, called Doppler radar, gathers information about wind speed and direction. Doppler radar also shows where rain is falling and how quickly the rain is moving. This can help scientists tell what path a storm might take.

▲ *Radar weather report*

Weather satellite ▶

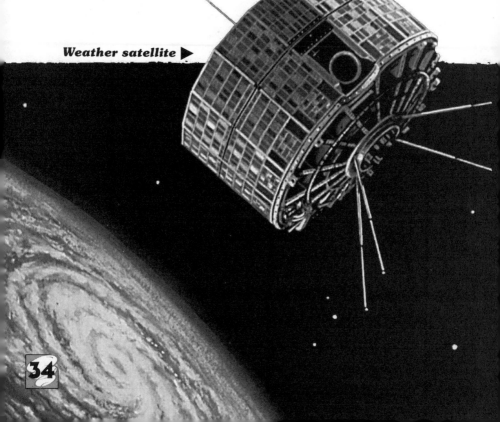

34

RADAR

Information gathered at weather stations and by satellites, radar, weather balloons, and other equipment is sent to computers. Meteorologists can then see what the weather will be around the world.

People hear what the weather will be through reports on television and radio. These reports help them plan their days. Even more important, they tell when a dangerous storm is on the way.

DID YOU KNOW?

Storm chasers have used small devices called Dopplers on Wheels to measure and map tornado winds. The radars are placed on trucks so they can follow a tornado.

Chapter

Being Prepared

No matter how carefully storms are watched, wind patterns are always changing. Storms can turn into tornadoes very quickly. This makes it hard to warn people. So it's important that people are always ready.

Listening to weather reports is the best way to find out about bad weather. A tornado watch means that a tornado could form. A tornado warning means that a tornado has been sighted by radar or a chaser.

Looking out the window and listening to the wind is also important. A tornado may be hidden behind rain and storm clouds. So people should watch for a very dark or strange-colored sky, hail, a loud roar, or a large, wall-like cloud. All are signs that should lead people to find a safe shelter.

Family watching storm report on television

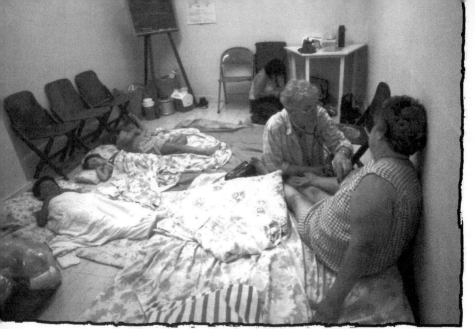

Red Cross shelter

The American Red Cross is a group that helps people during natural disasters. They suggest that every family have a home tornado plan.

First, a safe shelter should be chosen. If people live in a mobile home, they should leave and go to a stronger building or some other shelter. In a house, a good place to go during a tornado is the basement. The next best place is a hallway, bathroom, or closet near the middle of the lowest floor in the house. Everyone should stay away from windows, because they might break.

The Red Cross also says that families should keep these supplies in their shelter.

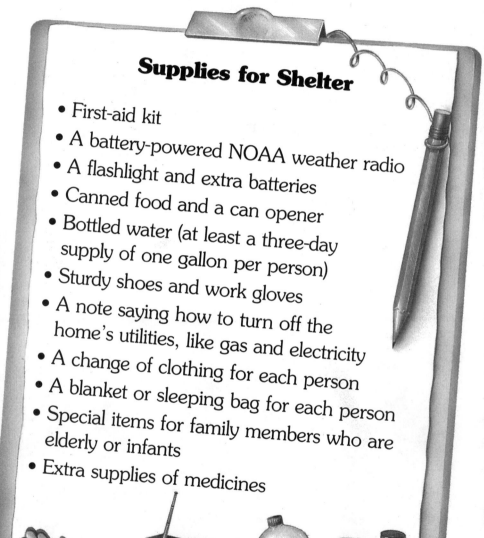

Supplies for Shelter

- First-aid kit
- A battery-powered NOAA weather radio
- A flashlight and extra batteries
- Canned food and a can opener
- Bottled water (at least a three-day supply of one gallon per person)
- Sturdy shoes and work gloves
- A note saying how to turn off the home's utilities, like gas and electricity
- A change of clothing for each person
- A blanket or sleeping bag for each person
- Special items for family members who are elderly or infants
- Extra supplies of medicines

In some places, tornadoes have become a way of life. Huntsville, Alabama, is one such city. Powerful twisters swept through Huntsville in 1974, 1989, and 1995. Winds as high as 300 miles per hour ripped up roads. Families found shelter as best they could. One family hid in a bathroom. Their house was wrecked, but they were safe.

After the last storm, the people who remained in Huntsville decided they needed to be ready for the next one. So, they rebuilt their city with tornadoes in mind.

Huntsville, Alabama, after a tornado

School tornado drill

    Almost every school, hospital, and business has a tornado plan. An outdoor warning system with fifty sirens was built. When the sirens go off, everyone can hear them.

    An elementary school that was destroyed in 1989 was rebuilt so that children would have a safe place to go to school. Part of the first floor is underground. There are no windows in the hallways or in the rooms. Every room is a storm shelter. The school holds drills so that the children and their teachers know what to do if a tornado comes.

Many people in Huntsville have built concrete shelters in the basement of their homes. In these shelters, they keep food, water, and other things they may need if a storm hits.

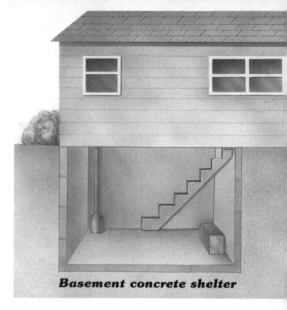
Basement concrete shelter

A trailer park outside town put in a big shelter under the ground. It can hold up to 1,000 people.

Chapter 7
After the Tornado

A tornado can cause a lot of damage. Homes and businesses may be destroyed. There may be no electric power or working telephones. After the tornado is gone, the real work begins.

Damage after a tornado

Rescue dog looking for survivors

Right after a tornado, search parties look for people who are missing. They sometimes use rescue dogs that can sniff out people in buildings that have fallen down. After tornadoes hit Florida in February 1998, rescue dogs found many people in the thick woods and brush.

The Red Cross brings disaster relief services to areas hit by tornadoes. It sets up shelters where families can sleep. It also gives people food and clothes.

Neighbors and business owners help each other, too. They help families look for belongings. They share equipment to start clearing away the debris.

Neighbors helping each other

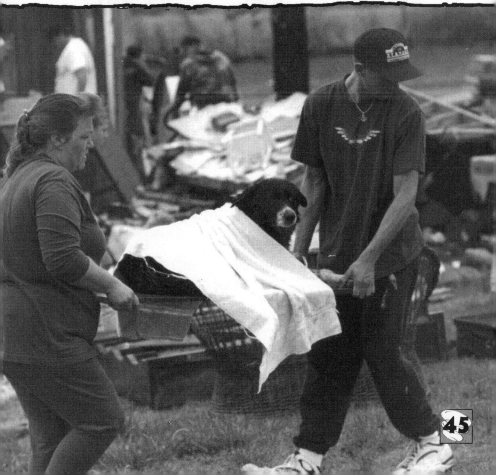

Jarrel, Texas - after a tornado ▲

The federal government and state governments also give money for disaster relief in the hardest-hit areas. This money helps towns repair or rebuild roads, schools, and hospitals. Money is also given to families to rebuild their homes.

Many communities hit by tornadoes start rebuilding right away. They know that life goes on after a tornado. It may take them months, and even years, to fix everything. But they won't let a tornado chase them away from their homes.

In time, life returns to normal.

Jarrel, Texas - after being rebuilt one year later ▲

As scientists learn more about tornadoes, with the help of storm chasers, they will hopefully be better able to predict when and where tornadoes will happen. Then people can better prepare their families and homes for a possible tornado.

DID YOU KNOW?

Before 1965, only two tornadoes had been filmed. Today, video cameras can capture tornadoes in progress. Scientists use video films to learn more about how tornadoes move and act.

Glossary

atmosphere (AT mus fihr) the layer of gases that surround Earth

damage (DAM ihj) the hurting or breaking of something

debris (duh BREE) waste material that is scattered about

disaster (dih ZAS tur) an event that causes damage and suffering

funnel (FUN ul) a tube shape that is wide at one end and narrow at the other end

meteorologist (meet ee ur AHL uh jihst) a scientist who studies Earth's atmosphere and predicts the weather

predict (pree DIHKT) to tell what you think will happen in the future

radar (RAY dahr) an instrument that sends out and picks up radio waves bounced off an object

satellite (SAT ul eyt) a small object made to travel around or orbit Earth

vortex (VOR teks) a spinning column of water or air